Caring for our Environment

Claire Llewellyn

W

FRANKLIN WATTS
LONDON · SYDNEY

This edition 2012

First published in 2009 by
Franklin Watts
338 Euston Road
London NW1 3BH

Franklin Watts Australia
Level 17/207 Kent Street
Sydney NSW 2000

Copyright © Franklin Watts 2009

Series editor: Julia Bird
Art director: Jonathan Hair
Design: Shobha Mucha
Consultant: Sam Woodhouse, Associate Consultant for
Geography & Citizenship, Somerset

A CIP catalogue record for this book is available
from the British Library.

Dewey classification: 363.7

Picture credits:
Alamy: 6: (t) © Manor Photography; 9: © Charles Stirling; 11: (t) © Alex Segre; (b) © Stan
Gamester; 12: (t) © June Green; 13: © Ian Miles/Flashpoint Pictures; 14: (m) © Sally & Richard
Greenhill; (b) © Jiri Rezac; 15: © The Photolibrary Wales; 16: © David Levenson; 17: © New
Zealand Stock; 19: (b) © Don Smith; 21: (t) © Photoshot Holdings Ltd; 23: © Blickwinkel; 25: (t)
© Jeff Greenberg; 26: (t) © Robert Harding Picture Library Ltd; (b) © Profimedia International
s.r.o; 27: (t) © Edward Parker; (b) © Doug Schneider. Corbis: p.24: (b) © Simon D Warren/Zefa.
Istockphoto: cover: (l) © Maciej Noskowski; 8: (t) © David Parsons; (b) © Tomasz Zajaczkowski;
10: (t) © Istockphoto; (b) © Arne Bramsen; 12: (b) © Istockphoto; 18: (t) © Monika Adamczyk;
19: (t) © Kais Tolmats; 20: (b) © Tony Campbell; 21: (b) © Lisa Thornberg; 22: (b) © Anne
Taylor-Hughes; 24: (t) © Kevin Eaves; 25: (b) © Andrew Howe. Shutterstock: cover (r) © Kuzma;
6: (b) © Chris Green; 7: © Kevin Eaves; 20: (t) © Arne Trautmann; 22: (t) Anatoli Dubkov;

Every attempt has been made to clear copyright.
Should there be any inadvertent omission, please apply to
the publisher for rectification.

ISBN 978 1 4451 0951 0

Printed in China

Franklin Watts is a division of Hachette Children's Books,
an Hachette UK company.
www.hachette.co.uk

Contents

What is the environment?

All the places and things that surround us are called our environment.

The school environment is made up of buildings, outside space, plants and air.

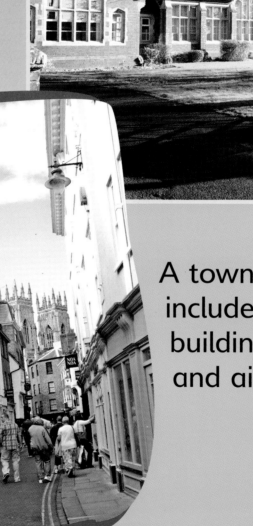

A town environment includes streets, buildings, plants and air.

A rural environment is made up of the land, streams, plants and air.

Sometimes people spoil
these environments.
How do they do this?
Turn the page to find out.

Spoiling th_ environm_nt

People spoil the environment in many different ways.

Cars and lorries make the air dirty.

People have dumped rubbish in this wood.

Look at this street. How has it been spoilt? How could it be improved?

Clean environments are good to be in. Spoilt environments are not.

Walk to School

Kalem walks to school every day.

He likes walking through the park.

He also likes going along the canal.

Kalem doesn't like walking along this road or past these boarded-up houses.

Why do you think he doesn't like these places?

What do you pass on your way to school?
What things do you like?
What things don't you like?

Cutting traffic

Too much traffic can spoil our environment. Many children travel to school by car.

The cars make the air dirty. They also make the road dangerous for people on foot or on bikes.

Pupils at one school set up a walking bus. Now lots of children walk to school instead of travelling there by car.

This has improved the local environment. The road is safer and the air is cleaner.

Does your school have a walking bus?

Noisy or quiet?

Noise also affects our environment. Too much noise is a nuisance.

Maxine uses a mobile phone to record the noise in different places around her school.

Hall

Playground

Classroom

Here are her results.

	Hall	Classroom	Playground

Which was the noisiest place?
Which place was the quietest?

Try recording the noise in different areas in your school. Where can you go for peace and quiet?

Pick up litter

Litter spoils any environment.

Tom's class went on a trip to their local park.

The park bins were all full. People had left their litter by the bin instead.

It made the park look messy and dirty.

The children wrote to the park manager about the problem.

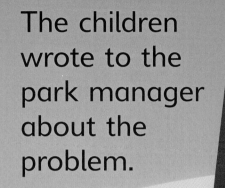

Dear Park Manager

We visited the park today and all the bins were full, so people had left their litter on the ground by the bins.

It made a real mess! We think the bins should be emptied more often so they aren't always full.

Can you help?

Thank you

Class 3C

The park manager has now arranged for the bins to be emptied more often.

Can you think what else we can do about litter? Turn the page to find out.

Reduce and recycle!

We can all reduce how much litter we make. For example, we can take food to the park in lunchboxes that can be used again.

We can also recycle some rubbish. Recycling means using old materials to make new things.

Waste paper can be collected at school or at home. It can be recycled into new paper.

Empty metal cans go in a can bank. They will be recycled into new cans.

Fruit, vegetables and old plant cuttings can be put into a compost bin. What do you think happens to them there?

What do you recycle at home?

Plants and the environment

Plants are an important part of our environment. They provide us with oxygen, which we breathe in.

They also provide wildlife with food and shelter.

No one cared for this piece of land. These children dug it and planted some seeds. It looks much better now, and provides food and shelter for animals and insects.

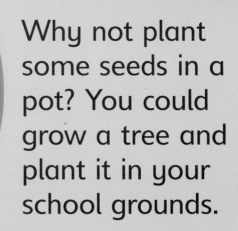

Why not plant some seeds in a pot? You could grow a tree and plant it in your school grounds.

Protecting wildlife

All plants create habitats for wildlife. Trees are home to squirrels, birds and many kinds of insect.

Which animals do you think might live among these reeds?

Wildlife needs our protection.
If we spoil or destroy habitats, the
animals that live in them will disappear.

Mark and Amy are building a pond in
their garden. It will be a habitat for insects,
fish and frogs. Birds will visit, too.

Could you create a wildlife habitat near
your home or school?

Special places

Our local environment is important to us. From time to time we visit other places, too.

Many people go hiking in the hills.

A forest is a great place for a picnic.

Beaches are very popular places.
This family is helping to keep the beach clean.

Wetlands are home to thousands of birds. People work hard to look after wetlands.

Caring for the planet

All over the world, people try to care for their own environments.

These cans have been recycled to make a door in Namibia in Africa.

In Holland, many people cycle rather than drive a car.

This girl is helping
to plant new trees
in the Amazon
rainforest.

This group
of boys are
cleaning up
a river near
New York in
the USA.

Our world is very beautiful.
If we take small steps, we can all
help to protect it.

Useful Words

Can bank – a place where empty metal cans are collected for recycling.

Canal – a waterway for boats that has been cut through the land.

Compost bin – a bin where rotting fruit, vegetables and plants can rot down into a crumbly mix. This is put on the soil to improve it.

Environment – everything that surrounds us.

Habitat – the place where a plant or animal normally lives or grows.

Improve – to make something better than it was.

Litter – rubbish that has been left lying on the floor or ground.

Materials – substances, such as glass and metal, that things are made out of.

Oxygen – a gas that is found in the air and which all animals need to breathe.

Rainforest – thick forest found in warm, wet areas.

Recycle – to turn old things into new materials.

Reeds – tall grasses that grow in shallow water.

Rural – in the country.

Spoilt – damaged so that it is dirty and unpleasant.

Walking bus – a group of children who walk to school together with an adult leader at the front and another adult at the back.

Wetlands – a low-lying, marshy area of land.

Wildlife – all living things, including plants and animals.

Some answers

Here are some answers to the questions we have asked in this book. Don't worry if you had different answers to ours; you may be right, too. Talk through your answers with other people and see if you can explain why they are right.

Page 9: The street has been spoilt because people have left litter on the pavement and in the road. People have also drawn graffiti on the walls. Picking up the litter and cleaning the graffiti off the walls would help to improve the street environment.

Page 11: Kalem doesn't like the litter or the boarded-up houses because they make places look ugly. No one cares about these places. This makes Kalem uncomfortable. He wonders whether these places are safe to visit.

Page 15: The playground was the noisiest place. The classroom was the quietest place. You could try going to the library for some peace and quiet.

Page 19: The fruit, vegetables and old plant cuttings will eventually rot down into compost in the compost bin. Compost can be put on the soil to help plants grow.

Page 22: The reeds are home to young fish and eels, beetles and snails, birds and water voles.

Index

About this book

This title, **Caring for your Environment**, is a way in for children to begin to understand the concept of the environment – a very topical and urgent issue which they will encounter in news programmes and so on. The learning in most of the activities is related to the National Curriculum section on 'Knowledge and understanding of environmental change and sustainable development'.
By working their way through the book, children will be learning the following **geographical skills**:

1. To recognise changes in the environment (National Curriculum 5a).
2. To recognise how the environment may be sustained and improved (National Curriculum 5b).

Learning content

As the children work their way through the book, they will also be learning the following **geographical enquiry skills**:
1. How to ask geographical questions (National Curriculum 1a).
2. To observe and record (National Curriculum 1b).
3. To express their own views about places and environments (National Curriculum 1c).

PSHE & Citizenship

Many of the issues are also related to the PSHE and Citizenship agenda for KS1 e.g. children will be recognising what they like and dislike, and to share opinions on things which matter to them; to realise that people and other living things have needs and that they have responsibilities to meet them (National Curriculum 2e) and about what harms their local environments and how to look after them (National Curriculum 2g).